To: _____

From: _____

This coupon book is my gift to you to thank you for being the world's greatest mom. These coupons never expire and are redeemable at any time by me. They are my special way of saying, "Mom, you're the greatest!"

World's Greatest Mom Coupons

SOURCEBOOKS, INC.®
NAPERVILLE, ILLINOIS

Published by Sourcebooks, Inc.
P.O. Box 4410, Naperville, IL 60567-4410
630.961.3900 Fax: 630.961.2168

Printed and bound in the United States of America
HS 10 9 8 7 6 5 4 3

Sourcebooks would like to thank the following individuals
for sharing their fun and creative coupon ideas…

Katie, IA   Jamie & Colby, CT   Debbie, TN
Madeline, WA   Jordan, KY   Meg, MN
Natalie and   Kara, MD   Brittany, MO
Melanie, IL   Heather, NY   Erin, NJ
Camille, CA   Melanie, FL   Miranda, TX
Crystal, OH   Kirsty, ME   Nicole, NC
Marissa, CA   Aubrie, CO   Kate, IN

Special Notes: _____

_____

_____

_____

_____

_____

_____

Because you are the World's Greatest Mom, I will tell you every day how much I love you!

Special Notes: _____

_____

_____

_____

_____

_____

_____

This coupon is good for one family bicycle ride

Special Notes: _____

_____

_____

_____

_____

_____

_____

Because you are the World's Greatest Mom, I will help you dust the furniture (but not the breakables!)

Special Notes: _____

_____

_____

_____

_____

_____

_____

*Let's make school
lunches together*

Special Notes: _____
_____
_____
_____
_____
_____
_____

*Because you are the
World's Greatest Mom,
I will unload the dishwasher
without complaining*

Special Notes: _____

_____

_____

_____

_____

_____

_____

Because you are the World's Greatest Mom, I will help dress my little brother/sister (or I will let my older brother/sister dress me)

Special Notes: _____

_____

_____

_____

_____

_____

_____

Instant coupon!
Let's shop for
school clothes

Special Notes: _____

_____

_____

_____

_____

_____

_____

Because you are the World's Greatest Mom, I will help you make cookies (you pick which kind!)

Special Notes: _____

_____

_____

_____

_____

_____

_____

This coupon entitles Mom
to a day free of cooking

Special Notes: _____

_____

_____

_____

_____

_____

_____

Because you are the World's Greatest Mom, I will help you pick a birthday present for Dad

Special Notes: _____

_____

_____

_____

_____

_____

_____

Because you are the World's Greatest Mom, I will help you cook dinner for a week (you choose the main course and I'll choose the dessert!)

Special Notes: _____

_____

_____

_____

_____

_____

_____

*This coupon is good
for a back rub*

Special Notes: _____

_____

_____

_____

_____

_____

_____

Because you are the World's Greatest Mom, I will be happy to do my homework

Special Notes: _____

_____

_____

_____

_____

_____

_____

Because you are the World's Greatest Mom, I will wash the dishes for one week

Special Notes: _____

_____

_____

_____

_____

_____

_____

*This coupon is good for
ten hugs and kisses*

Special Notes: _____

_____

_____

_____

_____

_____

_____

Because you are the World's Greatest Mom, I will serve you breakfast in bed

Special Notes: _____

_____

_____

_____

_____

_____

_____

*This coupon entitles
Mom to sleep in on the
day of her choice*

Special Notes: _____

_____

_____

_____

_____

_____

_____

Because you are the
World's Greatest Mom,
I will help you surf the Web

Special Notes: _____
_____
_____
_____
_____
_____
_____

*Because you are the
World's Greatest Mom,
I will write you a special
note you can carry
with you always*

Special Notes: _____

_____

_____

_____

_____

_____

_____

*This coupon is good for
one trip to the ice cream store*

Special Notes: _____
_____
_____
_____
_____
_____
_____

Because you are the World's Greatest Mom, I will write a thank you note to _____

Special Notes: _____

_____

_____

_____

_____

_____

_____

This coupon is good for one piece of fine art (made by me!)

Special Notes: _____
_____
_____
_____
_____
_____
_____

Instant coupon!
Get off the phone!

Special Notes: _____

_____

_____

_____

_____

_____

_____

Because you are the World's Greatest Mom, I will pick up my feet when I walk

Special Notes: _____

_____

_____

_____

_____

_____

_____

This coupon is good for one afternoon snuggle

Special Notes: _____

_____

_____

_____

_____

_____

_____

Because you are the World's Greatest Mom, I will draw you a picture or write you a poem to take to work

Special Notes: _____

_____

_____

_____

_____

_____

_____

This coupon is good for one beautiful bouquet of flowers

Special Notes: _____

_____

_____

_____

_____

_____

_____

Because you are the World's Greatest Mom, I will come home from a friend's house on time

Special Notes: _____

_____

_____

_____

_____

_____

_____

Because you are the World's Greatest Mom, I will not wander away from you when we go shopping

Special Notes: _____

_____

_____

_____

_____

_____

_____

Instant coupon!
Ask Your Father!

Special Notes: _____

_____

_____

_____

_____

_____

_____

Because you are the World's Greatest Mom, I will be nice to my brothers and sisters all afternoon

Special Notes: _____

_____

_____

_____

_____

_____

_____

Because you are the World's Greatest Mom, I will make my bed in the morning

Special Notes: _____

_____

_____

_____

_____

_____

_____

This coupon entitles Mom to listen to the music of her choice

Special Notes: _____

_____

_____

_____

_____

_____

_____

Because you are the World's Greatest Mom, I will let you choose the toppings on the next pizza we order

Special Notes: _____

_____

_____

_____

_____

_____

_____

Because you are the
World's Greatest Mom,
I will get the mail for you

Special Notes: _____

_____

_____

_____

_____

_____

_____

*This coupon entitles
Mom to a good nap
(minimum two hours)*

Special Notes: _____

_____

_____

_____

_____

_____

_____

Because you are the World's Greatest Mom, I will tell you what I did at school today

Special Notes: _____

_____

_____

_____

_____

_____

_____

Because you are the World's Greatest Mom, I will be glad to spend the night at my grandparents' house

Special Notes: _____

_____

_____

_____

_____

_____

_____

This coupon entitles Mom to one uninterrupted telephone call

Special Notes: _____

_____

_____

_____

_____

_____

_____

*Because you are the
World's Greatest Mom,
I will not cry or misbehave
when the baby-sitter
comes over to play*

Special Notes: _____

_____

_____

_____

_____

_____

_____

*Because you are the
World's Greatest Mom,
I will take one shower or
bath without argument*

Special Notes: _____

_____

_____

_____

_____

_____

_____

Send us your coupon ideas!

What do you most want to give Mom? Moms, what do you really want from your loved ones? Send us your coupon ideas—if we use them in our next book or in future editions, we'll send you a free copy of the finished book! Submission of ideas implies free and clear permission to use in any and all future editions. Send your coupons to:

Sourcebooks
Attn: Coupon Ideas
P.O. Box 4410
Naperville, IL 60567-4410

Other great coupon books from Sourcebooks

Best of Friends Coupons
Dear Daddy Coupons
Dear Mommy Coupons
Friends Forever Coupons
Girlfriends Coupons
Golf Coupons
I Love You Coupons
I Love You Dad Coupons
I Love You Grandma Coupons
I Love You Grandpa Coupons

I Love You Mom Coupons
Hole-in-One Coupons
Love Coupons
Romance Coupons
Sisters Coupons
Soothe Your Stress Coupons
True Love Coupons
Little Miracles—Coupons for
  New Moms and Dads
World's Greatest Dad Coupons